Wel World Little One

Judy Luca

Welcome to the
World Little One

Your journey here
has just begun

May you know that
you are loved

And always be
guided from above

when I see your
precious face

I know you can never
be replaced

From your head right
down to your toes

Let your body, mind
and spirit grow

May grace and wisdom
be with you

in everything
you say and do

May truth and faith
give you hope

Inspire you and help
you cope

Let joy and wonder
fill your days

As you grow
in glorious ways

May you be filled with
Radiant Light

Every day and
every night

Each day outshine the
morning sun

And share your love
with everyone

For you are a brilliant expression of Life

A splendid and truly Magical delight

Dedication

This book is dedicated to my first child Melissa. The first words I whispered to her when she was born were "Welcome to the world little one". She was crying but the moment I spoke she stopped and looked at me. It was truly a magical moment. Hope you enjoy sharing some magical moments reading this book to your little bundle of joy!

Copyright 2020
Judy Luca
All rights reserved
No part of this publication may be reproduced in any form or by any means, including scanning, photocopying, or otherwise without prior written permission of the copyright holder.

Made in the USA
Las Vegas, NV
20 October 2021